Shoulder

The Road to U.S.-European Military Cooperability

A German-American Analysis

DAVID C. GOMPERT
UWE NERLICH

Prepared for RAND Europe

RAND   IABG

CEAMA

Center for Euro-Atlantic Military Analysis

This research described in this report was sponsored by RAND Europe. The research was conducted through the Internal Security and Defense Policy Center (ISDPC) of RAND's National Security Research Division (NSRD).

ISBN: 0-8330-3209-7

Published 2002 by RAND
1700 Main Street, P.O. Box 2138, Santa Monica, CA 90407-2138
1200 South Hayes Street, Arlington, VA 22202-5050
201 North Craig Street, Suite 102, Pittsburgh, PA 15213
RAND URL: http://www.rand.org/
To order RAND documents or to obtain additional information, contact Distribution Services: Telephone: (310) 451-7002; Fax: (310) 451-6915; Email: order@rand.org

PREFACE v

SUMMARY vii

1 INTRODUCTION: CONCEPTS AND STRUCTURE 1

2 TOWARD THE PRAGUE SUMMIT: CAN IT ENSURE LONG-TERM
    COOPERABILITY? 9
    From Kandahar to Prague 9
    Strategic Options for the United States 12
    European Choices 14
    The Logic of a New U.S.-European Security Compact 17
    Turning Strategic Logic into Political Commitment 19
    A European Lead-Country Approach 21

3 COOPERABILITY OF TRANSFORMING FORCES: BROAD FRAMEWORK,
    SHARP FOCUS 25
    Three Military Missions in the New Strategic Environment 25
        Stability Operations 26
        Advanced Expeditionary Warfare 28
        Homeland Defense 28
    Three Force Categories 30
    Degrees of Cooperability 31
    Dimensions of Cooperability 33
    Cooperable Capabilities—Technical, Doctrinal, and Structural . . 34
    Preparing Cooperable Forces 35

4 WHAT THE UNITED STATES NEEDS FROM ITS EUROPEAN ALLIES FOR
    EXPEDITIONARY OPERATIONS 39
    Option 1: Contribute Throughout the Operation 40
    Option 2: Focus for Greatest Impact 43
    Evaluating the Options 45
    What European Capabilities Are Needed in Any Case? 46

5   Cooperability of German Forces with Transforming
    U.S. Forces 47
    The State of Bundeswehr Reform 48
    From Reform to Transformation 50
    A German Approach to Transformation 52
    Preliminary Ideas on Transformed German Capabilities 54

6   Getting the Process Right 57
    Why Current Processes Are Inadequate 57
    Concept Development and Experimentation:
      A Promising Avenue Toward Cooperability 60
    Implications for Institutions and Other Allies 63

7   Conclusions 67

PREFACE

This report is a product of the Center for Euro-Atlantic Military Analysis (CEAMA). In 1999, RAND and IABG established CEAMA for the purpose of reinvigorating transatlantic cooperation in defense research, which had languished since the Cold War ended. CEAMA conducts joint German-American analysis of obstacles to U.S.-European defense cooperation. Given its unique capabilities, as well as the special role the two parent institutions play in the United States and Germany, respectively, CEAMA is well qualified to conceptualize the challenge of U.S.-European military "cooperability"—i.e., the ability of U.S. and European forces to function together essentially as a single force with no loss in effectiveness—and to suggest a practical path for meeting that challenge.

The cooperability problem is the result of an interplay of complex forces: new global security challenges, U.S. and European responses to them, the power of distributed information systems, and the transformation of military forces to exploit the power of these systems to meet the new challenges. Therefore, the search for a solution must be broad, as this report's analysis is.

At the same time, prior efforts to improve cooperability have not succeeded in large part because they were unfocused. With this pitfall in mind, the paper spotlights a single process—*linking U.S. force transformation with that of the major European allies so as to become able to conduct advanced expeditionary warfare together*—as the key to cooperability. It calls for the United States and key European allies to make this the focal point of an urgent, determined, orderly, and sustained effort to ensure the military integrity and effectiveness of their alliance.

The authors have both immediate and long-term purposes for writing this report. In the short term, they hope its message will be absorbed by policymakers and defense planners who are wrestling with the problem of how to make best use of upcoming decision opportunities, such as the NATO summit to be held in Prague in November 2002, to get U.S.-European military cooperation and effectiveness on track. Beyond that, they hope to provide a framework for an enduring effort to create cooperable U.S. and European forces; for Prague, even if a great success, can be only a beginning.

Similarly, the authors hope to reach several audiences: policymakers, confronted with the here and now; defense planners, responsible for translating policy guidance into improved capabilities; the defense and international security research community, which has been stymied by this problem; and the broader, policy-minded public, interested in strengthening U.S. and European defense, the transatlantic partnership, and global security.

This research was conducted by RAND Europe jointly with the International Security and Defense Policy Center of RAND's National Security Research Division (NSRD), which conducts research for the U.S. Department of Defense, allied foreign governments, the intelligence community and foundations.

The CEAMA board members are

Klaus Naumann, Chairman (Germany)
Natalie Crawford (U.S.)
David C. Gompert (U.S.)
James McCarthey (U.S.)
Kzel-Adolph Neubecker
Uwe Nerlich (Germany)
Rudolph Schwarz (Germany)
James Thomson (U.S.)

Summary

The Cooperability Challenge

U.S. operations against Taliban and Al Qaeda forces have provided the first clear glimpse of the concepts, capabilities, and potential of military "transformation"—i.e., integrated forces exploiting information technology to gain comprehensive awareness and to operate in networks with speed and precise lethality against a bewildered enemy. Yet Afghanistan also shows that even the most capable U.S. allies, the Europeans, find it difficult to contribute to such advanced expeditionary warfare, while the United States seems reluctant to integrate allied forces lest they complicate already difficult operations. This gap in U.S.-European "cooperability"—i.e., in the ability of U.S. and European forces to function effectively as more or less a single force— was first revealed in Kosovo and is now so wide that NATO was unable to react militarily to a savage attack on one of its members.

The transformation of U.S. forces for expeditionary warfare is accelerating because of 9/11 and the ensuing defense spending hike. Meanwhile, allied force planning has focused on stability operations, mainly in or near Europe, which do not pose the sorts of severe challenges and dangers—such as weapons of mass destruction (WMD)—that compel force transformation. Because traditional forces cannot integrate and function effectively with transformed forces, the U.S.- allied cooperability gap is becoming unbridgeable, threatening basic U.S. interests, European interests, and the cohesion of the Atlantic Alliance.

Prior initiatives to upgrade European forces have not slowed this trend. NATO's Defense Capabilities Initiative (DCI) lacked a shared strategic motivation, a common military mission, and clear priorities. The European Union's European Capability Action Plan (ECAP) is aimed mainly at equipping and assembling European forces for stability operations, not warfighting; moreover, its chief purpose is European military autonomy, not U.S.-European military cooperability. Neither DCI nor ECAP is intended to transform forces for expeditionary warfare, in part because both have near-to-mid-term horizons, as opposed to a long-term one. What is needed is a major U.S.-European initiative, one that will begin transforming the forces of leading allies and will ensure their cooperability with transforming U.S. forces in advanced expeditionary warfare.

The New Convergence in Strategic Perspectives

Because of 9/11 and its aftermath, tackling the cooperability problem is not only urgent but also opportune. Well before 9/11, the United States was convinced of the need to be able to project power wherever its interests or responsibilities demanded, but most Europeans were not. At the same time, the United States was complacent about homeland security, while Europeans still thought of homeland security mainly in terms of a reconstituted threat from the East. Since 9/11, however, the United States and many allies have begun to think alike. The allies are beginning to accept U.S. thinking on the need to be able to wage expeditionary warfare wherever the need arises, while both they and the United States now understand that there is a homeland security problem—albeit a radically different one from the threat of Cold War years.

Still, the allies must decide whether they are serious about transforming their forces for the new type of expeditionary warfare. For its part, the United States must decide if it really would welcome allied forces in such operations if they were capable and cooperable.

It would be shortsighted for the United States to dismiss the military and political value of allied participation in power projection, as well as the potential harm to U.S. interests if the United States is left with no option but to wage war unilaterally. It would also be shortsighted for the allies to let themselves continue to drift toward total dependence on the United States to defend their interests militarily beyond Europe.

A Shared Framework

It is possible—and essential for pursuit of cooperability—to translate these newly convergent outlooks into a common U.S.-allied framework regarding military missions and required capabilities. Forces can be thought of as having three basic missions in the post-9/11 world:

- *Stability operations*, in which forces keep peace, tend to humanitarian needs, and perform other noncombat services in relatively permissive conditions.
- *Expeditionary warfare*, in which joint forces are rapidly deployed, conduct networked strikes to destroy enemy forces, and set the stage for stability operations.
- *Homeland defense*, in which forces selectively augment civil protection capabilities.

U.S. and allied force planning must address the requirements for all three missions. The United States is already preparing for the full spectrum, but European allies will have to broaden the scope and extend the reach of their planning to include expeditionary warfare in addition to stability operations. The alternative would be a strategic division of labor wherein the Europeans perform the missions designed to avert or restore order after conflicts in which U.S. forces do the fighting—a scheme that would serve the interests of neither Europe nor the United States in the long term and would violate a core principle of their alliance: shared risk.

The importance of U.S.-allied cooperability varies widely among the three basic missions. Cooperative national efforts will largely suffice in homeland defense. National units performing coordinated tasks under a single coalition commander are more or less adequate for stability operations. But for expeditionary warfare, forces must be integrated and virtually interchangeable, which is why forces not designed to meet similar warfighting requirements will not be cooperable.

Cooperability has several levels: physical capabilities, concepts of operation, command and control, preparations, and industrial-technological cooperation. The ultimate goal of a new transatlantic initiative should be to achieve cooperability at all of these levels for the mission in which cooperability is both most important and most challenging: advanced expeditionary warfare. And attaining cooperability for expeditionary warfare would effectively ensure that U.S. and allied forces are also able to perform well together in stability operations, which will remain a major mission for European forces. Although the United States has misgivings about being drawn into numerous open-ended stability operations, its leaders realize that U.S. forces must be able to contribute to them and to do so cooperatively with the forces of its European allies.

The keys to achieving cooperability are to initiate force-transformation planning among leading European force providers—the United Kingdom, France, and Germany, at least—and to couple that effort to U.S. force-transformation planning. If the forces of these "core countries" can gain cooperability with U.S. forces, it will help ensure that they are cooperable with each other's forces and eventually with other European forces. Although such a strategy would not depend on near-term reform of the NATO force-planning process, it would in due course restore NATO's effectiveness as a military alliance.

Linking U.S. and European force transformation would also give the EU much-improved capabilities and would avoid disharmony and maneuvering among the key force providers. Indeed, European Security and Defense Policy (ESDP) should be at least as committed to cooperability *with* U.S. forces as it is to the ability of Europe to operate *without* U.S. forces.

What the United States Needs, and What Leading Allies Might Provide

If allies are committed to both transformation and cooperability, they can eventually contribute substantially in coalition operations with the United States *if* they harmonize and pool their efforts. Although their individual operational roles and capabilities could vary, there are two basic, common options for allied roles in advanced expeditionary warfare:

1. *Joining U.S. forces in every major task throughout an operation*, including long-range strikes; rapid deployment of joint forces; tactical strikes on critical targets; gaining control of sea, air, and critical points of land; and destroying residual enemy forces in order to create conditions for successful post-combat stability operations.
2. *Concentrating on selective tasks for maximum military impact*, such as eliminating key anti-access capabilities (mines, WMD, air defense), employing special operations forces (SOF), participating in tactical precision strikes, mopping up enemy forces and command, and leading post-combat stability operations.

Of these options, the second has advantages for the Europeans. For the same level of resources, they can have greater military effect and more influence in operational and political decisions. Because of their specialization, they would have to sacrifice a measure of independence from the United States. However, it is unlikely that the allies would in any case have to wage expeditionary warfare without the United States, given where, why, and how such wars might need to be fought.

The second option also has advantages for the United States. Allies could augment U.S. forces in crucial tasks (such as overcoming anti-access capabilities) and could fill in gaps that would otherwise require greater U.S. investments (such as chemical, biological, and nuclear decontamination). Such interlocking capabilities would increase U.S. interdependence with allied forces, which the United States ought to be willing to do in the interest of military effectiveness and Alliance cohesion, provided, of course, that the allies are committed to building the necessary capabilities and making them cooperable.

Whichever the preferred option, key capabilities for the allies to obtain through transformation include fully interoperable C4ISTAR (command, control, communications, and computing; and intelligence, surveillance, target acquisition, and reconnaissance), long-range airlift, SOF, in-theater mobility, deployable ground forces, and diverse tactical strike forces (precision guided munitions, stealth, stand-off, aircraft, and sea-launched cruise missiles).

A European Approach to Transformation

To be able to provide cooperable capabilities, the leading European allies must

- Accept the need for their forces to be able to operate across the full spectrum of international missions and to do so with U.S. forces.
- Extend their force planning horizons beyond the near-and-mid term to the long term, so that they can better

anticipate emerging security risks, military operational challenges, and technological possibilities.

- Invest not only to correct known deficiences, but also to exploit new technologies that enable force transformation.
- Increase defense spending and streamline forces and structure of declining utility in order to fund transformational investment.
- Integrate new plans to transform their forces for expeditionary warfare with the continuing requirement to improve forces for stability operations.

Among the leading European force providers, Germany—because of the burdens of its history and politics—faces an especially complex challenge in adapting its planning process and its forces to achieve transformation and cooperability for expeditionary warfare. Germany's recent Bundeswehr Reform is an essential step in the right direction in that it orients the majority of German forces for international missions and corrects deficiencies identified in NATO and ESDP. It is essential that Bundeswehr Reform be implemented.

But it is equally critical that a substantial additional effort be made by Germany on the foundation of Bundeswehr Reform: plans, investments, and restructuring to transform a significant segment of German forces so that they can perform important coalition tasks in advanced expeditionary warfare wherever the need should arise. Such an additional effort by Germany would go far toward ensuring the cooperability of German forces with U.S. and other allied forces across the full spectrum of missions.

As Germany takes such steps (which would flow naturally from Bundeswehr Reform), a new and comprehensive framework for German defense in the new security era can emerge—a framework that encompasses and integrates stability operations, expeditionary warfare, and homeland defense. Germany's contributions to common security and international peace would grow, as would German influence in diplomacy, crises, and operations.

Getting the Process Right

Strong political commitments from both sides of the Atlantic, agreement on a common framework and priorities, and increased European defense spending—all of these are essential but not sufficient for achieving transformation and U.S.-allied cooperability. If momentum is to grow rather than fade, implementation is crucial.

The most important single initiative is that of tying key allies directly into the U.S. transformation process. It is the only sure way of achieving both cost-effective allied transformation *and* U.S.-allied cooperability. The specific mechanism in which such linkage is most important is concept development and experimentation (CDE). U.S. and allied force planners and military units, working side by side, would explore, learn, adapt, test, and refine concepts of operation and associated capabilities to transform not only as nations, but as a coalition—indeed, as an alliance. While procedures for this are already available, they must be expanded, intensified, institutionalized, and given sustained political attention.

There could be opposition in the United States to involving allies in such an important, sensitive, and already complex effort, just as there could be opposition in Europe to making U.S. transformation the turbine for European force planning. However, such opposition must be overcome if the Atlantic Alliance is to be militarily potent in the new era.

1 INTRODUCTION: CONCEPTS AND STRUCTURE

Although impressive operationally, the military campaign against Taliban and Al Qaeda fighters in Afghanistan has revealed deep faults in the strategy and capabilities of the Atlantic Alliance:

- The European political response to the 9/11 attack on the United States was swift and comforting, but there was no common Alliance strategy for coping with this new kind of challenge.
- Allies offered unreservedly to join in the immediate military response to the strikes, but U.S. forces carried out that response more or less unilaterally, owing both to the lack of European capabilities for such intense expeditionary warfare and to the U.S. reluctance to complicate an urgent, difficult operation.
- Because the United States wishes to limit the stay of its forces in Afghanistan, it is clearly pleased that able European forces are available for post-combat stability operations. Yet this pattern—United States fights, allies follow—only reinforces a trend toward a strategic division of labor that could undo the Atlantic Alliance.

Without doubt, the ability of U.S. and allied forces to cooperate in intense, violent contingencies without compromising effectiveness—i.e., their military *cooperability*[1]—is alarmingly low. While this has not prevented tactical success in Afghanistan, because the United States has in fact relied

---

[1]We use the term *cooperability* instead of the more common *interoperability* because the former connotes a broader and closer ability of forces from different nations to function together more or less as a single force, as opposed to separate forces that can interact.

little on allied forces in crucial combat actions, it has harmful implications for the respective roles, burdens, and risks of the United States and Europe in preserving international peace, for the relationship between them, and ultimately for their own security.

Despite voluminous analysis, finely worded communiqués, and well-meant initiatives, the facts show that neither the United States nor the European allies have made military cooperability a top priority. Nor is either sure what to do about it, especially now that the Americans have begun to transform their forces for advanced expeditionary warfare while the Europeans have not.

Difficult even in the best of circumstances, cooperability is virtually impossible between forces that have been transformed and those that have not. Transformed forces are highly integrated; are designed for speed, fluidity, and elusiveness; can be widely dispersed; and involve command and control doctrines that decentralize and encourage tactical initiative. Traditional forces cannot keep up with transformed forces, cannot integrate into their operating structures, cannot disperse without losing their effectiveness, and cannot adapt to more-distributed command and control doctrine.

What is so critical about force *transformation*? The main idea behind it is that information technology can be used to achieve a decisive military advantage by (a) networking forces, (b) giving them unprecedented operational awareness, and (c) enabling them to react far better than traditionally possible under fluid conditions. It thus opens a new chapter in the history of military affairs.

Even in the United States, transformation is a young endeavor. There is little hint of it in existing U.S. forces, which are still dominated by legacy weapons platforms and large single-service structures not designed for integration into joint forces for joint operations. As yet, it has had little impact on the information systems currently used by U.S. forces, many of which cannot "talk" to one another. Even the present official U.S. defense development and procurement program remains tilted mainly toward modernization of traditional capabilities rather than toward transformed capabilities. Notwithstanding top-level encouragement and impatience, U.S. force planners are struggling mightily to work through myriad obstacles—conceptual, technical, analytical, programmatic, institutional, and political.

Even so, U.S. transformation is now much more than a gleam in the eye. It has become the spirit and organizing principle for change. As inertia grudgingly surrenders to innovation in U.S. defense policy, transformation will have a defining effect on U.S. force structures, operating doctrines, investments, and capabilities. Even in its infancy, its stunning effects can already be seen in the unprecedented networking, awareness, precision, and reaction times of U.S. forces in the rugged terrain of Afghanistan—an example that is already spurring yet more rapid and sweeping transformation.

U.S. force transformation is being driven not only by technological opportunity but also by global security demands. The United States anticipates rising difficulties and perils, to its forces and to its homeland, in waging *expeditionary warfare* against adversaries with anti-access capabilities (e.g., mines and air defense) and means to reach the United States. These adversaries range from hostile states (like Iraq) to sophisticated terrorist groups (like Al Qaeda); their capabilities may well include weapons of mass destruction (WMD)—chemical, biological, radiological, and nuclear. Challenges could erupt in deserts, mountains, jungles, or urban concentrations. U.S. concerns about such dangerous enemies and circumstances are distributed around the rim of Asia, from Korea to Taiwan to Southeast

Asia to the Indian subcontinent to the Persian Gulf to the Arab-Israel conflict.

Meanwhile, security problems within the European region, although still of concern to the United States, are not so severe that they demand transformed forces. Ethnic feuds still simmer around Albania, but they are growing less likely to require NATO to wage large-scale combat operations, much less to involve any danger of WMD use or any risk of large casualties among U.S. and allied forces or populations. Rather, future military contingencies in Europe are most likely to call for *stability operations*—e.g., peacekeeping and peace enforcement—which involve, at worst, semi-permissive conditions and for which traditional (untransformed) forces are adequate. Most European allies are only now, since 9/11, beginning to accept the need to confront the sorts of global dangers that are propelling U.S. force transformation—dangers that could also hit Europe or vital European interests. Consequently, the U.S.'s militarily ablest allies, the Europeans, have fallen behind the United States in contemplating, let alone implementing, transformation.

Given the acceleration of U.S. transformation, the obstacles and preoccupations in U.S. transformation planning, and the fact that Europeans have barely begun to focus on the global dangers that motivate transformation, it should come as no surprise that the European allies, and thus the Atlantic Alliance, are late to reach the starting line. It is not too late, but it soon could be.

To be fair, U.S. hesitation about allied participation in Operation Enduring Freedom was based on considerations of military effectiveness, not indifference, arrogance, or divergence of interests, as some pundits claim. American commanders, for good reason, were concerned that the integration of allied forces might retard or degrade combat operations. Thus, very real effects of the Europeans' late start in transforming their forces have already occurred. Such effects will grow exponentially if cooperability is not made an urgent strategic priority on both sides of the Atlantic.

Afghanistan shows that the absence of cooperability can preclude coalition expeditionary warfare even when the United States and its European allies are of one mind strategically, as they were after 9/11. This absence did not prove decisive in Afghanistan, but it could in the event of, say, a major conflict in the Persian Gulf, where a genuine coalition operation would be imperative for political and perhaps military reasons.

There is also a danger that not having cooperable forces will accentuate the divergence in American and European strategic orientations that caused the gap to open in the first place. Even though cooperability does not guarantee U.S.-European strategic harmony, its absence can negate the value of such harmony in a military crisis. That in turn could erode the harmony itself. It is all too easy to foresee a downward spiral for the Atlantic Alliance.

Neither cooperability nor transformed forces are ends in themselves, of course. Yet the United States and its allies have not seriously discussed, let alone agreed upon, what ends they seek and what military missions those ends might demand. Therefore, the pursuit of cooperability between transformed U.S. and European forces should be guided by, and help precipitate, a broad transatlantic consensus on why such capabilities are needed.

Achieving cooperability will require that Europeans accept responsibility to prepare for and join in expeditionary warfare, with its costs and risks, wherever and whenever the need arises. It will require that the United States opt for coalition operations (and strategies) over unilateral operations (and strategies). And it will require that Europeans and the United States develop a shared conception of why and how they may have to use force—shoulder to shoulder—in the service of peace, security, common interests, and common values.

Such a shared conception must encompass the entire expeditionary mission spectrum: stability operations (of all sorts), advanced expeditionary warfare (of all sorts), and the many ways either one can lead to the other. While different in character and in the kinds of capabilities required, these two basic international missions are interwoven:

- Expeditionary warfare will usually lead to a requirement for stability operations, as it did in Iraq, Kosovo, and Afghanistan.
- It could also be that a stability operation will fail and lead to a need to wage war, as it did, in a way, in Bosnia.
- Expeditionary warfare and stability operations could overlap in time and even in territory, as has occurred in Afghanistan.

For these reasons, decisions to undertake combat operations need to anticipate the requirements for post-war stability operations, just as stability operations should be viewed in terms of their escalatory risks and the possible need to resort to deadly force. The idea that the United States can handle expeditionary warfare by itself and leave stability operations to its European allies, or vice versa, is a recipe not only for political divisiveness but also for operational confusion and possible calamity. It also ignores the ambiguities and uncertainties that soldiers and strategists must learn to respect in this highly fluid new security environment.

Stability operations can also serve fundamentally important security purposes from which the United States cannot dissociate itself and instead count entirely on its allies. By the same token, the Europeans are courting serious and potentially disastrous dependence on the United States by letting their lack of transformed forces require the United States to conduct expeditionary warfare by itself. Given both these broader security implications and the close situational connections between stability operations and advanced expeditionary operations, it follows that *both the United States and at least the major European allies ought to be able to perform both types of missions, and to do so in coalition.*

Cooperability is obviously a complex issue. It involves questions of strategy, capabilities, structures, operational concepts, preparations, technology, and shared decision-making—not to mention sovereign interests and the roles of different multilateral institutions. The Prague summit cannot possibly settle all these questions. But it can make a new beginning. Now is the time to face up to the issues of U.S. force transformation, allied force transformation, U.S.-European cooperability, and the full spectrum of expeditionary military missions—and on that basis to start the process of generating solutions that ultimately can give NATO new life as a military alliance.

Alternatively, if the United States and at least the leading European allies do not decide on a framework and work plan now, cooperability can only become harder to achieve. Why they should have a stronger motivation or better opportunity in the future than they do now is unclear. The Alliance may be approaching not only its best chance but also its last.

The urgency with which the cooperability problem needs to be tackled plus the complexity of doing so requires a program for action based on a shared framework. This report attempts to set forth that program by answering a sequence of questions:

1. What is the nature of the cooperability problem and why, from U.S. and European perspectives, must it be addressed?

2. Is there a *common* way (post-9/11) to express the security interests, military missions, force needs, and cooperability aims of both the United States and the Europeans?
3. What cooperable capabilities, to perform what missions, should the United States seek from its European allies?
4. What capabilities should one leading country—Germany—develop to advance both transformation and cooperability?
5. What transatlantic processes are needed to facilitate cooperability?
6. What should be the highest priorities for agreed-upon practical implementation?

If we, the authors—one American, one German—have been able to generate agreed-upon answers to these questions, there is hope that the United States and its European allies can do so as well.

2 TOWARD THE PRAGUE SUMMIT: CAN IT ENSURE LONG-TERM COOPERABILITY?

In the aftermath of Operation Enduring Freedom, both the United States and its principal European allies are confronted with a new reality:

- Amidst the formation of an impressively broad anti-terrorist coalition, leading European nations offered their military support to the United States, only to discover that, even collectively, they had little to contribute to the fast-breaking complex combat operation that ensued.
- Following the first invocation in history of Article V (the NATO Treaty's collective defense provision), it became painfully clear that NATO had no role to play in defending the United States against its attackers in Afghanistan.[2]
- The European Union's (EU's) rapid reaction force could not have helped—even if it existed.

Five years ago, the Kosovo war exposed a wide gap between U.S. and allied capabilities. Now, the Afghanistan operation has shown that NATO could not respond as a military alliance to a savage attack on one of its members, owing to the inability of the Europeans and the reluctance of the United States to conduct expeditionary warfare together.

From Kandahar to Prague

The current situation is all the more chilling when one bears in mind that the major European allies had already con-

---

[2]The need to reform NATO's political and military apparatus goes well beyond cooperability and thus the scope of this report. However, other reforms will make little difference if cooperability is not achieved.

cluded over the past decade that expeditionary operations have replaced traditional territorial defense as the object of NATO and European military strategy. In recent years, two major force-modernization efforts were meant to improve allied capabilities:

- NATO's Defense Capabilities Initiative (DCI) sought to spur and choreograph European military modernization measures in order to improve both the Europeans' expeditionary capabilities and their cooperability with U.S. forces. However, DCI lacked a common strategic orientation, provided no doctrinal and institutional links to the U.S. force-transformation process, set no priorities, and failed to inspire allied investment in force modernization.
- In parallel, the EU's European Capability Action Plan (ECAP) was intended to improve European *collective* capabilities. However, it was not aimed either at force transformation or at U.S.-European cooperability.

Both DCI and ECAP were meant to produce near-to-midterm improvements in European forces, not a long-term solution to the divergence in U.S. and allied defense strategies, doctrines, and capabilities. Neither DCI nor ECAP has led to increased European defense spending. And neither has bridged nor, as conceived, *can* bridge the ever-wider, ever-deeper cooperability gap.

Given the intensity and scale of the U.S. military transformation effort, especially after 9/11, the NATO summit in Prague is shaping up as a critical moment to begin building that bridge. Unless it becomes preoccupied with enlargement, Prague will be, in NATO Secretary General Lord Robertson's words, the "Capability Summit." As such, it will face a steep challenge: It is patently clear from the Afghanistan experience that NATO is not now functioning effectively either in ensuring the cooperability of its members' forces or in waging war in its members' defense.

While the United States still leads NATO's force-planning process, that process has become sclerotic and increasingly disconnected from the U.S. national force-transformation process since the end of the Cold War. The force goals NATO suggests for its members have become a faint echo of old needs. The more demanding and dangerous the expeditionary operation—especially outside Europe, where security dangers are most acute—the *less* likely that NATO will be involved. In sum, NATO can neither prepare for nor conduct precisely the sort of military operations that will be most crucial for the security interests of both the United States and the European allies. Whatever its other virtues— e.g., as a U.S.-European consultative forum or as a means of engaging former enemies in the East—a NATO that cannot project decisive, collective power where and when the interests of any of its members require is an impotent military alliance.[3]

Afghanistan leaves unanswered two key questions:

- Are the European allies truly committed to transforming their forces to conduct expeditionary warfare wherever the need may arise?
- Is the United States really willing to integrate allied forces into expeditionary warfare if they are made capable and cooperable?

In other words, *are the European allies committed to taking more global security responsibilities, and is the United States committed to coalition warfare?* If the answer is no on either count, cooperability will remain a mirage—and NATO, as a military alliance, could become a memory. However, if the United States perceives its allies as being

---

[3]An impotent military alliance is not likely to be of much use in the long run as a forum for security consultations among the United States, the traditional European allies, and former Cold War adversaries.

serious about building forces capable of advanced expeditionary warfare, *and* the Europeans perceive the United States as genuinely willing to integrate capable allied forces in coalition warfare, the effect will be mutually reinforcing. Therefore, before considering how to achieve cooperability, it is necessary to consider whether cooperability is deemed imperative on both sides of the Atlantic.

Strategic Options for the United States

Even without the huge U.S. budget increases following 9/11, cooperability in expeditionary warfare would have continued to decline, because the United States had already set a course of transformation and the allies had not. The nearly $50 billion increase in defense spending, because it provides additional resources to transform U.S. forces, will heighten the cooperability challenge even further.

Why should this matter to the United States? With its unrivalled military power and potential, the United States could opt for go-it-alone strategies in confronting the principal global security challenges, allowing its European allies, like its other friends, to become less and less relevant to the policies, crises, operations, and outcomes of meeting these challenges. Alternatively, the United States could encourage a strategic division of labor, one in which U.S. forces conduct decisive, high-tech warfare while European allies perform *stability operations*[4]—which U.S. planners view as open-ended, costly, high-risk, low-tech, and having high manpower requirements, and for which current and programmed European forces are actually designed and more or less adequate. Together, Operation Enduring Freedom and the heavily European follow-on stability operation in Afghanistan could set a regrettable precedent for such a division of labor.

---

[4]In this report, the term *stability operations* refers to military activities meant to contain and lower the risk of war, as opposed to those meant to defeat an adversary with deadly force.

Would either the go-it-alone or the division-of-labor option serve American interests? After all, if U.S. force transformation makes unilateral operations increasingly certain of success at an acceptable cost in lives, treasure, and public support, why does the global superpower need an unwieldy multilateral coalition for expeditionary warfare? The answer lies in the basic approach that the United States has taken to the rest of the world since emerging from isolation in the middle of the last century. In the wake of two successive world wars, the U.S. attitude has been "to foster a world environment in which the American system can survive and flourish."[5] This attitude is no less correct today, irrespective of U.S. military superiority or the growing problem of U.S. and European cooperability. Indeed, the immense U.S. stake in today's integrated world economy arguably makes multilateralism more compelling than ever. The United States should want responsible and capable partners, as well as effective security institutions, precisely because the sharing of U.S. values and interests fosters the "U.S.-friendly" environment sought after World War II.

In contrast, unilateralism could turn the planet into an increasingly hostile, lonely environment for U.S. interests. It could turn the United States into a resentful global constable, insensitive to the concerns of even its closest friends. Moreover, for all its resources, the United States needs allies to help shoulder global burdens—assistance that, according to all opinion polls, the U.S. public overwhelmingly appreciates.

If the United States must wage war unilaterally because the neglect of cooperability has left it with no alternative, *especially* in the most demanding and dangerous circumstances, it could find itself with increasingly inequitable risks to its forces and to its homeland—risks that could become

---

[5]National Security Council, NSC 68: *United States Objectives and Programs for National Security*, Section VI, Part A, first paragraph, April 1950.

disproportionate to U.S. interests and to Americans' sense of international duty. The United States would bear the brunt of international scorn toward its solo use of force, however unfairly. And it would see its principal alliance—the product of its genius and leadership—atrophy. Even the division-of-labor option fails the test of serving long-term U.S. interests, because it splits the risks and consequently the policies of the United States from those of its allies.

Perhaps the American people will not recoil from lonely burdens, thankless risks, and singular vulnerability. But if they do, global peace and U.S. security interests will surely suffer. Therefore, if the United States does not presently have faith in even its ablest allies to join it in projecting power, the right U.S. policy should be to fix the problem, not dismiss it.

European Choices

European allies may be hesitant to accept greater burdens and sacrifices to achieve cooperability in power projection unless they clearly sense that the United States would welcome their military involvement. The Europeans need to know what the United States considers to be useful combat forces and whether it is predisposed to combine such forces with its own in coalition warfare. They will want to know, as well, whether increasing their capabilities and contribution will correspondingly increase their influence in crisis diplomacy and wartime decisionmaking. Thus, a clear U.S. commitment to coalition crisis management and coalition expeditionary warfare is a prerequisite for the Europeans' willingness to transform their forces and make them cooperable with U.S. forces.

Even with an unambiguously positive American disposition, however, European allies may still feel they are better off leaving the warfighting, with all its military and political perils, to the United States. There remains considerable political sentiment in Europe in favor of confining European forces to stability operations, such as peacekeeping and humanitarian relief, preferably in or near Europe. This bias for low-end, permissive, noncontroversial, nearby operations could constrain the Europeans' willingness not only to join in high-intensity combat but also to invest in the requisite capabilities to do so.

For European politicians, the option of continuing to concentrate on low-violence stability operations, and correspondingly less-expensive capabilities, is naturally tempting. But as the events since 9/11 show, it is an option that will demolish their ability to influence crisis diplomacy. It will deepen the Europeans' dependence on the United States to protect European interests, as *it* sees fit, from global terrorism, regional aggressors, WMD and other dragons of the new era.

For better or worse, the U.S. logic of war and peace—and of warfare itself—will prevail as long as U.S. allies lack advanced, cooperable forces. This is hardly acceptable as an enduring condition for Europeans. And the Europeans' complaints about U.S. unilateralism, about U.S. quickness to use force before other options are exhausted, and about the way the United States wages war will all ring hollow to U.S. ears until allied forces have the capabilities needed for cooperability with U.S. forces.

If leading European nations choose to confine themselves to stability operations, this will also tend to encourage intra-European divergences. Certain nations might seek to gain privileged positions vis-à-vis the United States, though without the capacity to field significant capabilities on their own. Influence on the United States would thus remain marginal, and intra-European competition, suspicion, and maneuvering would grow. Under such divisive conditions, European Security and Defense Policy (ESDP) would fail, with grave consequences for EU cohesion and self-respect; and NATO itself would be no more than a U.S.-dominated organization for handling lesser crises in and near Europe, crises that may not even involve U.S. vital interests—a sure recipe for losing interest in the Alliance on both sides of the Atlantic.

European nations thus face a strategic choice that is starker than they like to admit: a choice between preparing only for stability operations and preparing for the full spectrum of military operations, including expeditionary warfare as well as stability operations. If they choose the latter path, their forces *must* be cooperable with those of the United States, since they and the Americans are far more likely than not to be together in any crisis so severe that expeditionary warfare is warranted. At the same time, the Europeans would also be better prepared to conduct combat operations under EU auspices in the unlikely but not implausible circumstance that the United States is not involved.

A choice by Europeans to transform their forces would thus strengthen not only U.S.-allied military cooperability and NATO, but also ESDP capabilities and EU cohesion. It would surely strengthen the emerging U.S.-EU relationship, which could be the core security partnership in global security in the 21st century.[6]

Because it confronts the need to be able to fight wars abroad, the path of transformation and cooperability will be more expensive and more controversial than the current path for the Europeans in the short term. But the current path would prove more costly by far in the long term. While a lot is at stake for all Europeans, this is particularly true for Germany. Of the major European force providers, Germany is the most reliant on strong, functioning multinational security institutions, especially NATO and the EU.

[6] A rationale and a blueprint for a U.S.-European strategic partnership—global and equal—were first set out in David C. Gompert and F. Stephen Larrabee (eds.), *America and Europe: A Partnership for a New Era*, New York: Cambridge University Press, 1997.

The Logic of a New U.S.-European Security Compact

Obviously, we are convinced of the need for European force transformation and U.S.-European cooperability. In the end, however, the prospects for such developments will depend on whether the United States and the European allies have convergent underlying strategic viewpoints and motivations. Although U.S.-allied cooperation in the Afghanistan combat operations has not been encouraging, we believe there is a basis for hope that a new, post-9/11 convergence will appear.

Well before 9/11, the United States was committed to fulfilling its international security responsibilities and defending its interests by being prepared to project decisive military power wherever and whenever required. At the same time, the United States was complacent about its homeland security, not having been vulnerable since the 19th century (except for the deterred Soviet nuclear force). While U.S. defense analysts have conjectured for some years that it was only a matter of time before adversaries, including terrorists, would respond to U.S. expeditionary capabilities by striking directly at the United States, the country was unprepared, physically and psychologically, for 9/11.

In contrast to the United States, European allies have experienced direct threats to their homelands for much of the past century. The main rationale for NATO, after all, was to multilateralize the defense of Germany from Soviet invasion. After 1989, Germany felt "surrounded by friends" but regarded with alarm the outbreak of conflict nearby in the Balkans. The Gulf War showed that vital European interests could be threatened far abroad.

Nevertheless, the general pre-9/11 European sentiment was that European security needs and responsibilities could be satisfied by performing peacekeeping and other stability operations in and on the outskirts of the European region.

Threats of the sort that would require rapid, decisive expeditionary warfare elsewhere were well over the allies' geographic and time horizons—America's business. In sum, U.S. and allied strategic orientations were divergent before 9/11.

Since the 9/11 terrorist strikes, Americans and Europeans have *both* recognized that they must prepare for new threats to homeland security—for the United States, a *new* experience; for the allies, a type of threat very *different* from that of territorial invasion. In parallel, 9/11 has prompted Europeans to consider assuming greater responsibility for dealing with international insecurity wherever it erupts, not only with peace operations, but also with combat operations. It has made the ESDP's Petersberg Tasks, which were artfully vague about whether they included expeditionary warfare anywhere in the world, a parchment for the archives.[7]

More specifically, 9/11 has strengthened the case for transforming U.S. forces to deal with a full spectrum of dangers. It emphatically closed the book on the U.S. method of planning its forces solely to fight "major theater wars" (MTWs).[8] Finally, it showed that accepting unilateral international security responsibilities could expose the United States more than other nations to homeland threats.[9]

As the leading European allies now contemplate conducting combat operations away from Europe, they too must face up to the need to transform their forces for effectiveness against rising dangers. Transformation is not a peculiarly American idea that U.S. allies must embrace solely for fear of being marginalized. Rather, it is the pathway to a way of warfare that exploits information technology in order to

---

[7]There is in fact a growing sense within the EU that the Petersberg catalogue needs to be reconsidered and redefined to provide greater clarity and more attention to warfighting missions.

[8]The new U.S. force-planning construct stresses decisive action and versatility across a wide spectrum far more than the 2-MTW standard.

[9]Osama bin Laden has been clear that U.S. military presence in Saudi Arabia is his *casus belli.*

achieve battle awareness in the face of uncertainty, to make forces less vulnerable to increasingly dangerous weapons, and to operate with unprecedented speed and precision. The post-9/11 world makes transformation as important, on its own merits, for Europeans as it is for the United States.

The new strategic convergence (see Table 1) suggests that an opportunity exists for a common assault on the increasingly acute problem of U.S.-European military cooperability. The question is whether statesmen and strategists will grasp the logic and convert it into policy.

Turning Strategic Logic into Political Commitment

The upcoming Prague summit will have to cope with a complex set of issues if it is to produce genuine and lasting success.[10] The United States needs to embrace the concept that coalition operations are better than going it alone, even—indeed, especially—in intense expeditionary warfare. It will have to be prepared to accept certain compromises that are sure to be controversial at home: joint decisionmaking with participating allies in crisis diplomacy; strategic and tactical intelligence sharing; allied involvement in the U.S. force-transformation process; advanced technology sharing.

To be clear, however, the quest for cooperability is no reason for the United States to slow the transformation of

Table 1—U.S. and European Strategic Outlooks After 9/11

	U.S.	European Allies
International security demands	From MTWs to full spectrum	From Petersberg Tasks to full spectrum
Homeland security	A threat exists	A *different* threat exists
New defense priorities	Accelerate transformation and build homeland defense	Begin transformation and reorient homeland defense

[10]By definition, all NATO summits "succeed" in producing impressive communiqués and photo ops of determined, united leaders. All too often, however, success dissipates rapidly.

its military, which would be a grave mistake for U.S., European, and global security. Indeed, slowing the U.S. transformation is not necessary to restore the ability of the United States and its allies to wage advanced warfare together. U.S. resolve to transform does not endanger or preclude cooperability; allied failure to transform does. If European allies can be connected to the U.S. transformation process, it can be the locomotive of both European transformation and U.S.-European cooperability.

Therefore, European nations should seek to link up with the U.S. force-transformation process—a goal entirely compatible with their common EU defense aspirations. And, of course, they need to invest adequately in creating capabilities and force structures that will enable military integration with U.S. forces in advanced expeditionary warfare.

U.S. transformation, while well under way, has a long-term orientation—roughly, 2015–2020. The huge post-9/11 budget increase should facilitate transformation by providing resources to fund new investments without stripping current capabilities, thus also reducing bureaucratic and political opposition to change. Nevertheless, the road is a long and unmapped one, even for the United States, since the doctrinal and structural changes needed fully to exploit new technology will take a generation to make.[11]

European nations have yet to discover the virtues of long-term transformation goals (although the successful evolutionary history of the EU might have taught them such virtues). Lately they have focused more on joining existing European forces into an EU rapid reaction force than on developing new capabilities. But there is time, provided a commitment is made now, before the U.S.-European cooperability gap and the accompanying strategic divergence become unbridgeable.

---

[11]For example, improving the deployability of ground forces without compromising their lethality will require the development, production, and fielding of a "Future Combat System" by the U.S. Army, replacing the main battle tank (which is too heavy). This process will take at least two decades.

Because they cannot be expected to increase defense spending as dramatically as the United States has just done, the Europeans will find the tension between transformation requirements and traditional needs difficult to manage financially and institutionally. However, some European allies (e.g., Germany) still have large forces suitable only for defense against an invasion threat that has not simply receded but vanished altogether. Thus, while increased European defense spending is clearly needed, there are opportunities to mine resources from forces of diminished utility in order to finance investments in transformation.

A European Lead-Country Approach

Unlike the United States, which has the capacity to provide capabilities for both stability operations and advanced expeditionary warfare, no European ally is able *by itself* to meet the needs of both missions. Nor will the EU, as such, be in a position in the foreseeable future to make and carry out political commitments that cover both requirements. For the time being, major European countries—those that are the main force providers and have relatively broad defense industrial-technological bases—need to coordinate their planning and pool their resources in order to effect transformation, meet both stability and warfighting requirements, and achieve cooperability with the United States.

Without the United Kingdom, France, and Germany, no such effort can succeed. And unless these three leading European allies proceed more or less in step, there will be too many opportunities for divergence, maneuvering, and, in the end, inadequate capabilities. A number of other European nations—such as Sweden, Italy, Spain, and the Netherlands—could also move in this direction.

The United Kingdom, France, and Germany all have near-to-mid-term military reforms under way to address the fluid challenges of the new security environment. Each has its own force-planning approach, reflecting sundry national, NATO, and ESDP demands, and each is struggling to find sufficient resources for modernization.[12] So some foundation stones exist on which to build.

Just how far the force planning, reforms, and modernization of these three major European force providers have progressed is an important variable in any strategy to transform and attain cooperability with the transforming U.S. forces. Progress in updating doctrine, structure, and capabilities has certainly not been wasted. However, two factors have greatly impeded European progress toward transformed capabilities.

First, as already mentioned, there are insufficient resources, aggravated by a tardiness to discard outdated capabilities. Since dramatic budget increases cannot be expected in the near term in any of the three countries, irrespective of who governs them, current reforms, while essentially on the right track, are not enough to effect transformation. Not only will transformation have to be made an unambiguous long-term goal, but the resources to achieve it will have to come largely from bolder efforts to pare capabilities and structures that no longer contribute to security.

Second, planning for stability operations does not confront defense establishments with the severe operational challenges that expeditionary warfare so rudely poses: rapid deployment with little warning; overcoming anti-access threats, including WMD; integrating strike-and-maneuver operations to destroy critical targets, including mobile and concealed ones; real-time sensor-to-soldier information.

To achieve cooperability with transforming U.S. forces, European allies must put in place their *own* long-term trans-

[12]Germany was the first to seize upon 9/11 as a reason to increase defense spending. The United Kingdom also makes a case for increased spending in the "New Chapter" to its *Strategic Defence Review*. (See UK Ministry of Defence site, specifically www.mod.uk/issues/sdr/new_chapter/.)

formation process, rather than merely shadowing American moves. The requirements of this European process are

- As noted, a strategic motivation that is as broadly compatible as possible with that of the United States.
- Some common understanding of how current forces and programmed investments for stability operations relate to new requirements for advanced expeditionary warfare.
- A long enough planning horizon to exploit emerging technology and to make enabling changes in structure and doctrine (e.g., 2015–2020).
- Operationally derived capabilities requirements.
- Concept development and experimentation (CDE) to go beyond mere analysis of the deficits of current forces.[13]
- A structured process that combines top-down guidance, bottom-up creativity, and purposeful resource allocation.
- Collective transformation commitments, at least among the leading force providers.
- Measures for tracking progress.[14]

At every level and phase, it is essential for U.S.-European cooperability that the allies have their own transformation process *and* that the allies and the United States work to connect their respective transformation processes. The next chapter sketches a framework that could be shared by the United States and the major European allies for structuring and prioritizing "cooperable transformation."

---

[13]The problem with deficit analysis, whether in connection with DCI or ECAP, is that it rarely gives rise to new concepts to solve military operational challenges, tilting instead toward more or incrementally better versions of present capabilities.

[14]The U.S. Defense Department is still struggling with the problem of how to measure transformation progress. Therefore, an opportunity exists to develop common measures, from which the United States would also benefit.

3 COOPERABILITY OF TRANSFORMING FORCES: BROAD FRAMEWORK, SHARP FOCUS

Let us assume that both the United States and the leading European allies are determined to restore cooperability through linked transformation. In that case, they will need a *shared framework* within which agreed-upon undertakings can be implemented and measured. As noted before, DCI lacked a long-term orientation, strategic coherence, a tight link to U.S. transformation plans, and a sense of priorities; and ECAP included neither transformation nor U.S.-European cooperability among its goals. This next, and perhaps final, effort must have these missing elements.

Accordingly, we offer here a policy framework to which both the United States and the European allies should be able to subscribe—one that would give order and focus to their efforts to transform their forces in tandem and thus achieve cooperability.

The framework starts with a basic question: *Why do the United States and the major European allies need military forces?* While the American answers will, of course, vary in detail from those of the Europeans, as will the answers of one European country vary from another, we believe that there is more common ground than has been recognized to date and that it can furnish a motivation, framework, and program for cooperable transformation.

Three Military Missions in the New Strategic Environment

The convergent strategic logic described in Chapter Two distinguishes between international security and homeland security. These two elementary purposes are interconnected: Acceptance of international responsibility may lead to homeland vulnerability, failure to confront international dangers could allow threats to the homeland to grow, and failure to provide homeland security undercuts the credibility of intervention to ensure international security. However, the two purposes imply quite different military missions, operational tasks, and therefore doctrines and capabilities.

International security demands could occur across a wide spectrum, from humanitarian deliveries under permissive conditions, for example, to large-scale, intense expeditionary warfare under extremely dangerous conditions. For purposes of force planning, this spectrum can usefully be divided into two types of missions: *stability operations* and *advanced expeditionary warfare*. While the reasons for this distinction will become clear below, suffice it to say here that the first of these two basic missions does not demand force transformation, whereas the second does.

Homeland security, as noted, concerns the protection of a nation's infrastructure and institutions, its economic health, and the confident safety of its citizens from new threats, including large-scale terrorist attacks, perhaps involving WMD. The basic military mission associated with homeland security can be thought of as *homeland defense*.

Because these three basic missions are, since 9/11, recognizable to both European and U.S. planners, setting capability requirements to fulfill them could be part of an agreed-upon framework for cooperability. But this depends on a deeper understanding of each mission.

Stability Operations

Military stability operations are usually defined in terms of their objectives—e.g., show of force, humanitarian intervention, peacekeeping, or peace enforcement, with or without the potential for escalation. Such operations could be intended to avoid war (Macedonia), could deteriorate into war (Bosnia), or could follow war (Kosovo). In Afghanistan, stability operations and expeditionary warfare overlapped, underscoring the need to plan and manage each in light of the other. A key campaign goal of expeditionary warfare could be to create conditions in which stability operations can be effective and safe. Conversely, stability operations that are attempted before such conditions exist could be fraught with problems and dangers, as was found by UNPROFOR (the United Nations Protection Force) in Bosnia and has been recently witnessed with Operation Anaconda in Afghanistan.

Stability operations can be demanding, lengthy, costly, risky, and politically unrewarding. Because they are usually conducted under tight rules of engagement and delicate political circumstances, they can also be very difficult, which explains why NATO forces and commands are increasingly favored over UN-run operations. Performing such operations well can, of course, make the difference between war and peace. Failure to mount effective stability operations could allow victory to descend into renewed hostilities. The Balkan and Afghan experiences demonstrate that even major European force providers are not yet fully prepared for this mission, especially in terms of transport, surveillance, and command and control. It is all the more difficult to conduct effective post-war operations when countries that have not been involved in the warfighting phase inherit the results.

As important as such missions may be, for the leading European force providers to confine themselves to stability operations will place them in a precarious position: responsible for potentially unstable results from a crisis they did not manage, a war whose outcome they did not affect, and prior decisions they did not make. This is one reason the division-of-labor option looks as bad for Europe as it does for the United States.

For their part, U.S. forces have frequently participated in stability operations and have displayed considerable competence, albeit at large costs in consumables, troops over-used, and warfighting readiness compromised. The United States is, at best, ambivalent about participating in stability operations. However, most U.S. policymakers understand that a U.S. role could be militarily or politically indispensable in some cases and therefore cannot be excluded. For U.S. planners to assert that U.S. forces exist *only* to "fight and win the nation's wars" or that U.S. allies should handle stability operations is to encourage an unhealthy division of labor and to leave the United States unprepared for an uncertain future.

Advanced Expeditionary Warfare

The new threat environment may require the projection of deadly force employing innovative operational concepts, superior capabilities, and even unorthodox tactics to achieve decisive military results at minimum casualty levels. With hostile states and groups able to acquire WMD, anti-access capabilities, and long-range delivery means, expeditionary warfare will become increasingly problematic and dangerous in the absence of transformed concepts and capabilities—which, again, is precisely why the United States is strongly motivated to transform.

Sometimes called "rapid decisive operations," such advanced expeditionary warfare is a new experience for the United States and an altogether unfamiliar one for the European allies. After a decade of halting progress, the United States appears at last to be on track in planning and preparing for such warfare. In contrast, European nations are still planning for more-traditional operations. Consequently, even though U.S. force transformation is still only embryonic, Operation Enduring Freedom allowed little opportunity for European military contributions.

Homeland Defense

There is, since 9/11, a third basic military mission, which is completely new for the United States and very different from previous missions for European nations: homeland defense.[15] While not all European countries will be directly exposed to the new strategic terrorism, those that play large roles in the "Western" political, economic, and security systems will. The United Kingdom, France, and Germany are probably second only to the United States as likely targets. Moreover, these countries are the most likely to participate in coalition expeditionary warfare in areas of concern to strategic terrorists (e.g., the Middle East and Persian Gulf), making them potential targets of those terrorists' counter-intervention strategies. In any case, the growing integration of Europe—on its own and within the world economy—will increase the transnational effects of terrorist attacks in any European nation.

Homeland defense presents new military tasks, mainly in support of civil security and emergency-response organizations, for both the United States and Europe. It is, above all, a national responsibility; indeed, organizing it is proving to be a major challenge to existing national governmental structures.[16] However, in view of similar experiences, common threats, and cascading transnational effects, U.S.-European coordination will be beneficial. It is not in the interest of any member of an expeditionary coalition for any other member to be so vulnerable to homeland attack that it could weaken coalition cohesion, effectiveness, and nerve.

All aspects of homeland security—including military homeland defense—for the United States and the European allies would benefit from a continuous exchange of data, plans, and know-how. Intelligence sharing regarding terrorist networks, strategies, and intentions is imperative. Old-fashioned swapping of information—"We'll show you what

[15]The broader concept of *homeland security* includes law enforcement, information network protection, aviation security, and many other efforts that do not involve the use of military forces.

[16]Within the EU, 9/11 has triggered beginings of what could become an internal EU security community, depending on the extent to which the European Commission is given a role.

we have if you'll show us what you have"—will not do. Efforts to gather, interpret, sift, and present intelligence data should be as common as possible, within the limits of security.

Critical, vulnerable infrastructure can range from national to virtually global. Because information networks are especially transnational, protecting them goes beyond the capacity of any country. Aviation safety, container safety, food safety, disease control, and the protection of energy flows and nodes all require at least collaborative if not integrated efforts.

With the possible exception of ballistic missile defense, homeland defense does not require high cooperability of U.S. and European military forces.[17] For the most part, reserves, not active forces, will provide backup support to civilian organizations. And their tasks will tend to be very local.

Three Force Categories

Because the three basic missions significantly differ from one another in military operational terms, they require different *packages* of capabilities. Briefly put, stability operations require mainly light ground forces with modest lethality, good mobility and sustainability, and C4ISR (command, control, communications, and computing, and intelligence, surveillance, and reconnaissance),[18] and air control. Advanced expeditionary warfare demands the ability to bring superior forces and precision strikes to bear suddenly from any domain, direction, and distance so as to degrade enemy capabilities and will, to gain complete control, and to eliminate the enemy's ability to fight again. Homeland defense requires auxiliary military support for civil agencies.

---

[17]Cooperability in ballistic missile defense is relevant to both homeland defense and advanced expeditionary warfare. Because the need will arise first in expeditionary warfare—for force protection—we address it there.

[18]Target acquisition (TA) is less crucial here.

To say these packages of capabilities differ is not to say the actual forces for them must be mutually exclusive. From a U.S. perspective, most of what is required for stability operations will be subsumed in the capabilities for advanced expeditionary warfare. If the major European allies are to be able to conduct advanced expeditionary warfare, they will have to add substantial new capabilities, as just described, beyond what they now have or are planning for stability operations. Each major European ally must not only transform its forces, but also make them available to a combined capability.

Generally speaking, using expeditionary forces for a homeland defense mission would run a potentially intolerable risk that an enemy will threaten homeland attacks precisely to divert expeditionary forces and perhaps avert intervention. Moreover, the concepts and capabilities called for by expeditionary operations are sufficiently dissimilar to those needed for homeland defense to suggest that quite different forces are required for these two missions. As a corollary of this, reserve forces that are to be used in homeland defense should not be designed or earmarked to reinforce forces in expeditionary warfare.

Similar capability requirements, based on similar missions, are preconditions for cooperability between U.S. and European forces. Efforts to improve technical compatibility, doctrinal harmony, joint preparations, industrial collaboration, and institutional harmony depend on this.

Degrees of Cooperability

Cooperability is not binary but, rather, a matter of degree. The degree of cooperability required varies by basic mission (see Figure 1). Homeland defense can benefit from coordination and, in selective aspects, common effort. Stability operations require close collaboration among national military units with a common purpose, related tasks, and a single top commander. To be effective, multilateral expedi-

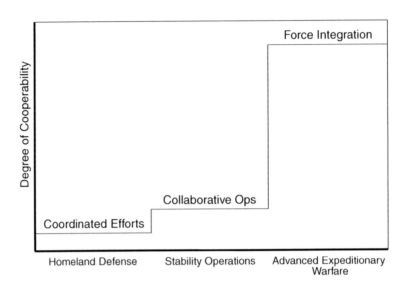

Figure 1—Degree of Cooperability Required for Three Missions

tionary warfare requires integration of forces that have already been made compatible, if not interchangeable, in doctrine, capabilities, and joint preparations.

Thus, the more intense and dangerous the operation, the more integrated the forces must be and the greater the need for cooperability. Strategically, U.S.-European cooperability is the most important for expeditionary warfare because of the likely high stakes of such operations—the restoration of international peace, the defeat of aggression, the safeguarding of common vital interests (e.g., energy supplies), action against strong and fanatical terrorist cells, etc.

Therefore, *the highest priority must be given to achieving the most difficult yet most vital level of cooperability: that required for advanced expeditionary warfare.* This will virtually assure needed cooperability in stability operations, where the tempo is slower and the dangers and uncertainties are fewer. There are also selective opportunities to improve homeland defense through cooperability, though they are beyond the focus of this report.

Dimensions of Cooperability

Cooperability has been associated with technical compatibility. This is not wrong, but it is incomplete. As essential for cooperability, and more elusive than technical compatibility, are common concepts of operations (CONOPS) at the campaign and tactical levels. The current transformation of U.S. forces and the needed transformation of European forces are as much about CONOPS as about equipment.

Closely related to both technical and doctrinal cooperability is compatibility in the way forces are structured for operations. U.S. joint forces—air, naval, and ground forces integrated at the small-unit level—will not be able (or willing!) to operate with, say, a nonmodular allied ground-force division.

Another crucial dimension of cooperability, as well as of transformation, is the ways in which forces are prepared for operations: experimentation, simulations, training, and exercises. These preparations are essential in testing and incorporating new doctrine, technology, and structures; in identifying and repairing weaknesses; and, of course, in getting ready for "co-operations."

At another level, the defense industrial-technological bases of the United States and Europe can help or hinder cooperability, depending on how they are shaped by U.S. and European markets, policies, and defense industrial politics.[19]

Table 2 shows the cooperability requirements for the three basic missions. The message reinforced here is that the focus of cooperability efforts must be on advanced expeditionary warfare (with attention also to selective aspects of homeland defense). Cooperability is both more challenging

---

[19]This report does not delve into the many issues and layers of U.S.-European and intra-European defense industrial/technological policies. Suffice it to say that military cooperability is best served by a transatlantic defense-systems and technology market that is open and competitive but also collaborative.

Table 2—Cooperability Requirements, by Mission

Requirement	Stability Operations	Advanced Expeditionary Warfare	Homeland Defense
Technical	Medium	High	Selective
Doctrinal	Medium	High	Low
Structural	Medium	High	Low
Preparatory	Low	High	Selective
Industrial-technological	Low	High	Low

and more crucial at the high end of the operational spectrum.

Cooperable Capabilities—Technical, Doctrinal, and Structural

The United States already possesses, is building, or is designing every important capability needed for distant, rapid, decisive combat:

- Long-range airlift
- Intelligence, surveillance, target acquisition, and reconnaissance (ISTAR)
- Interoperable command, control, communications, and computing (C4)
- Diverse and robust precision strike (any range, stealth, missiles, stand-off, land-/sea-based)
- Unmanned airborne vehicles with sensors and/or weapons (unmanned aerial vehicles [UAVs] and unmanned combat air vehicles [UCAVs])
- Deployable, mobile, sustainable ground forces—lighter but still lethal
- Special operations forces (SOF)
- In-theater mobility

- Information operations (IO)
- Deployable missile defense (ballistic and cruise).

In addition, the United States is experimenting with how to organize its forces to use these capabilities to best effect in integrated joint operations. Although retarded by institutional inertia and interservice rivalry, the trend is toward more modular, smaller units that can be tailored and integrated for seamless joint operations. The United States is, in parallel, considering the creation of standing joint force elements to speed the process of assembling a total joint force for an expeditionary warfare contingency.

Chapter Four suggests in some detail what allied force contributions the United States might welcome from its European allies for advanced expeditionary warfare. Chapter Five sets out what force contributions one particular ally—Germany—might opt to make. At an absolute minimum, European capabilities for advanced expeditionary warfare must include a core consisting of interoperable C4ISTAR, tactical precision strike, deployable ground forces (including SOF), and strategic and in-theater mobility. The allies need not have equipment identical to each other's or to that of the United States. But they should have shared CONOPS, structures that can be integrated, compatible technical standards, and a common interoperable C4ISTAR grid.

Achieving cooperability for this core set of capabilities, at each of the five levels shown in Table 2, should set the agenda for European-U.S. cooperability. This agenda will require not only investments in and restructuring of capabilities, but also collaborative preparations.

Preparing Cooperable Forces

A critical aspect of transformation, in conjunction with clarifying requirements and aligning investments, is preparing forces. Preparations begin with exploratory analyses of innovations and culminate with getting forces ready for actual operations. If this is critical for the forces of any one country, it follows that it is critical to harmonizing forces from several countries whose cooperability is important.

Preparations are needed to permit new doctrines, tactics, and alternative ways of organizing forces to be thoroughly investigated. This is especially crucial at a time when innovative use of information technology in network-centric warfare—a key concept in transformation—is just beginning. Preparations are also tests, intended to reveal deficiencies and indicate adaptations. They enable forces of different services and/or countries to become accustomed to operating in integrated ways with command, control, and communications.

The United States and lead allies should make preparations a matter of the highest priority in their cooperability strategy. They should develop bilateral and multilateral programs that include

1. *Computer simulation models* involving current and alternative allied capabilities and threats, to help reveal cooperability problems and test solutions.
2. *Concept development*, to stimulate fresh thinking about how to solve operational challenges.
3. *Experimentation*, to evaluate concepts and to learn together.
4. *Combined training*, to bolster familiarity and effectiveness.
5. *Command exercises*, to strengthen C4ISR.
6. *Crisis-management games*, to improve coalition decision-making.
7. *Full-scale exercises*, to test, prepare, and demonstrate the cooperable capabilities of the coalition.

It is the nature of the transformation process that feedback from all such preparations can be invaluable in requirement setting, investment, and force structuring. This iterative loop should be built into the U.S.-European process for achieving cooperability (see Chapter Six).

Improved and collaborative force planning is imperative if cooperability is to be achieved. Even for the United States, ensuring robust forces capable of performing both stability operations and expeditionary warfare is proving to be a challenge in force planning and resource allocation. For core European nations that may be just now embarking on force transformation to meet expeditionary warfare requirements, the challenge will be more difficult still. European force modernization has traditionally had a short-to-medium-term horizon (out to ten years or so). However, full exploration of how emerging technologies might solve anticipated operational problems needs a longer time horizon (15 years and beyond), as do the changes in doctrine and organization these technologies enable. To the extent that cooperability with transforming U.S. forces is to become a force-planning criterion for European nations, long-term planning will become essential.

In sum, traditional planning approaches will suffice to meet stability operations requirements, which are evolutionary and can be based on recognizing deficits between current needs and current capabilities. But if the European allies are to transform their forces for advanced expeditionary warfare, they will need to

- Make long-term planning an integral part of force planning
- Make cooperability with transforming U.S. forces a planning goal
- Prepare top-down guidance (e.g., defining strategic and key operational challenges)
- Intensify their own bottom-up research on expeditionary warfare concepts and capabilities.

4 WHAT THE UNITED STATES NEEDS FROM ITS EUROPEAN ALLIES FOR EXPEDITIONARY OPERATIONS

Let us assume that

- The United States rejects both the *go-it-alone* and the *division-of-labor* options, choosing instead to seek the participation of capable forces of leading allies alongside its forces even in the most demanding expeditionary warfare.
- Leading allies accept, in principle, the need to transform their forces for such operations and to attain cooperability with U.S. forces.
- As a consequence, the Prague Summit produces a genuine commitment to restore the military coherence and effectiveness of the Atlantic Alliance by activating cooperability efforts at every level (as indicated in the previous chapter) needed to conduct advanced expeditionary warfare as a coalition.

Under these assumptions, a critical question leaps out: *What specific military roles should European allies play in advanced expeditionary warfare?*

The answer is, of course, up to the European allies. However, they will want to know what preferences the United States has, based on the military and political demands of such operations and on the challenge of integrating U.S. and allied forces into a cohesive force. Although we do not know how the United States would respond officially to this question, we can at least illustrate its significance.

The starting point for considering possible U.S. views on specific allied roles is a rather detailed understanding of the main operational challenges that need to be met to succeed in advanced expeditionary warfare, whether by U.S. forces alone or by forces of a U.S.-led coalition. While every campaign will be unique, the chief operational challenges will usually include[20]

- Extending C4ISTAR over the prospective operation
- Conducting long-range strikes against anti-access capabilities
- Deploying tactical forces with unprecedented speed (a few days)
- Gaining control of sea, littoral, air, space, and cyberspace
- Attacking/seizing critical land points with fast-maneuvering forces
- Eliminating residual offensive and anti-access capabilities
- Providing critical support, including escalation control, to post-conflict stability operations.

In view of these challenges, there are two interesting options for allies: one in which they play roles *throughout the operation*, and one in which they concentrate on tasks through which they can have the *greatest impact on the operation*. The choice between these two approaches will have a huge impact on allied force plans and investments, cooperability efforts, operational plans, crisis management, command arrangements, outcomes, and the relative independence of both the United States and the European allies.

Option 1: Contribute Throughout the Operation

The United States may see advantages in having the forces of its most able allies participate from the outset and continuously throughout an expeditionary war. Such an approach would ensure that the risks, both to forces and to homelands, are more or less evenly shared and that the rest of the world is able to see that the United States is not using force unilaterally. All else being equal, a more multilateral operation from start to finish might be viewed as a more

---

[20]One should be cautious about assuming or planning a particular sequence of these tasks, since every campaign is different. However, the listed order is a plausible, if highly simplified, sequence.

"legitimate," supportable operation.[21] Allies would help by augmenting U.S. capabilities throughout, but their participation would not be militarily indispensable to any main task or to the final outcome.

In this option, European forces could have a role in each of three phases:

- Join in early strikes to *degrade* the adversary's anti-access capabilities and thus create favorable conditions for the engagement of tactical forces.[22]
- Rapidly (e.g., by air) deploy tactical strike and ground forces to the theater to help *gain control* of the littoral, airspace, cyberspace, and critical points of land.
- *Eliminate* critical targets (e.g., missile launchers, WMD sites, elite forces, command and control, logistics hubs) to render the adversary unable to continue fighting or unable to pose dangers to stability operations and regional security.

More specifically, allied forces might join U.S. forces in carrying out any of the following important tasks:

- Maintain peacetime military presence in areas of potential or impending crisis
- Strike suddenly from any range
- Eliminate air defenses, mines, missile launchers, WMD
- Degrade enemy C4ISTAR
- Deploy tactical air, naval, and ground forces rapidly to any distance
- Insert SOF in hostile territory
- Take and keep control of sea, littoral, air, and cyberspace
- Mount quick-response strikes on critical (mobile) targets from air and sea

[21]The U.S. campaign in Afghanistan, though not broadly multilateral, was deemed legitimate almost universally because it was an unambiguous act of self-defense.

[22]Physical or electronic.

- Insert land forces networked with strike forces to seize critical points of land
- Finish off enemy forces that could threaten post-war stability operations.

As U.S. transformation proceeds, U.S. forces performing these tasks will become increasingly fast, aware, lethal, precise, and integrated. Integration will erase military-service boundaries, spatial domains, and nonessential hierarchy. Therefore, if allied forces are to operate with U.S. forces throughout an operation, they will have to be more or less equally as capable *and* integrated quite deeply into the U.S. command structure.

Bluntly put, the United States will not welcome allied forces that lack either the capabilities or the degree of integration that enables them to keep pace, conduct critical tasks, and operate seamlessly with U.S. forces in combat. For example, allied aircraft that can neither strike with precision from extended range nor reliably penetrate advanced enemy air defense cannot be counted on for critical early strikes against other anti-access capabilities. This is purely a matter of operational efficacy and safety.

What capabilities would allies need to carry out key tasks throughout an entire operation?

- Long-range airlift (in large numbers)
- Offensive and defensive information operations
- SOF
- Rapidly deployable, light, lethal, mobile ground forces
- In-theater mobility for forces and logistics
- Long-range strike platforms
- Stand-off precision munitions
- Penetrating tactical strike aircraft
- Surface-to-surface missiles

- Missile defense interceptors and battle management systems
- Interoperable C4ISTAR.

This is a major undertaking in terms of needed allied capabilities, integration and subordination of allied forces within U.S. command, and the preparation needed to be able to conduct rapid and seamless coalition operations under great uncertainty—ranging from long-term planning to exercises.

These capabilities could more easily be fielded if the leading European allies pooled their investments and their forces for full-spectrum expeditionary warfare. Already, under ESDP, they are planning to pool capabilities. However, as noted above, the current ESDP plan is skewed toward European stability operations and is not meant to ensure U.S.-allied cooperability in advanced expeditionary warfare. Therefore, if the European allies expect to participate broadly, effectively, and on a meaningful scale with U.S. forces in advanced expeditionary warfare, they will have to redefine ESDP to foster both transformation and cooperability.

To the extent the Europeans spread their efforts across the entirety of a large-scale expeditionary operation, their military impact will be diffused. Moreover, the investments required to transform European forces for all tasks will either demand much greater spending or result in wide but shallow capabilities.

Option 2: Focus for Greatest Impact

The second option is for the European allies to concentrate on key roles that will complement U.S. strengths or fill U.S. shortfalls so as to have a more decisive effect on critical tasks and thus on campaign outcomes. This approach would increase the military value of allied participation, though it would also leave both the United States and the allies more vulnerable if one or the other opts out of an operation. It might also, depending on details, mean that U.S. forces would not be joined by coalition forces throughout an entire campaign.

Specific tasks in which allies might play an especially consequential role include

- *Rapid airborne deployment of mobile ground forces.* The United States is far from being able to dispatch a large ground force by airlift, both because of shortage of airlift and because most of its ground forces remain too heavy to be airlifted.[23]
- *SOF.* Not even the United States will find it easy to maintain these elite forces in very large numbers, as Operation Enduring Freedom has shown. Allies have selective SOF on a par with U.S. capabilities. As seen in Afghanistan, SOF are highly joint, versatile, and transformational, particularly when networked with sensors and strike assets.
- *Diverse tactical strike.* Although Europeans need not contribute to long-range strike—which is becoming a very high (and very expensive) U.S. priority—they could contribute to the intensity and diversity of tactical strike. This task requires stand-off and penetrating, land- and ship-based missiles and aircraft. Stealth could become indispensable as enemy air defenses improve. Tanker capacity is needed to enable tactical-range aircraft to reach distant theaters.
- *Ballistic and cruise missile intercept.* European allies could participate in and augment U.S. intercept capacity using U.S. or shared sensors and common battle management systems.
- *Chemical and biological detection, prevention, and decontamination.* This task remains an Achilles heel even

---

[23]Emphasis on airlift capacity is, of course, also in line with European defense industrial goals.

in advanced expeditionary warfare. Allies can be as capable as the United States in improving and expanding these capabilities.

- *In-theater mobility.* As with long-range airlift, the United States, given its own needs, will not be able to move allied forces or supplies swiftly throughout the theater.

The capabilities required for these more selective tasks would be a subset of those needed in option 1. However, greater depth and sophistication would be needed, and presumably possible, given the chance to concentrate resources. The case for the core European allies to pool and coordinate their contributions is just as strong in this second option as in the first. Of course, the need for the Europeans to reach agreement on their respective coalition roles would be both more critical and more difficult.

Evaluating the Options

Table 3 indicates which allied option—contribute throughout an operation or focus on tasks having the greatest impact—seems superior for different criteria, and provides a brief explanation for each choice.

On the whole, option 1, in which the allies broadly emulate U.S. capabilities, would leave the United States and the Europeans comparatively independent, whereas option 2, which is the more interlocking approach, would accept interdependence in the interest of coalition military strength. Option 2 could also give the Europeans benefits in influence and defense industrial/technological competitiveness.

This result, while only indicative, is quite significant. It suggests that the single-minded pursuit of *independent* European capabilities would be *dis*advantageous in a number of respects one would expect to be of great importance to the allies: military impact, political and policy influence, and industrial vitality.

Table 3—Rating of Two Options for Allied Role

Criterion	Option 1: Contribute Throughout Operation	Option 2: Focus for Greatest Impact	Explanation
Cost		✓	Selectivity saves money
Military impact		✓	High-impact tasks
European autonomy	✓		Broad capabilities
European influence		✓	Critical roles
U.S. autonomy	✓		Minor dependence
Defense industry		✓	Greater depth

What European Capabilities Are Needed in Any Case?

From any perspective and for either option, a certain core set of capabilities will be required of allies hoping to play a significant role in U.S.-led advanced expeditionary warfare:

- Interoperable C4ISTAR
- Long-range airlift
- In-theater mobility and logistics
- Advanced tactical strike (stand-off, stealthy penetration, and precision guided munitions [PGM] capabilities)
- Mobile, lethal ground forces (including SOF).

5 Cooperability of German Forces with Transforming U.S. Forces

At the heart of our recommended strategy is a European "lead-country" approach. These lead countries—the United Kingdom, France, and Germany, at least—occupy a pivotal position, for each needs to have military cooperability along three dimensions:

- With transforming U.S. forces
- With each other's forces
- With the forces of other European allies and partners, old and new.

This is a tall order for defense leaders and force planners in the lead countries. However, by linking their own force planning to the turbine of U.S. transformation, the lead countries can start and sustain their own transformation, thus improving their own capabilities, the effectivness of U.S.-European coalition operations, and ultimately the military integrity of the Atlantic Alliance. Further, by playing a leading role in Europe—in due course linking their transformation to that of other European allies—they can enable the EU, through ESDP, to become an effective force for international security in its own right. Thus, a strategy of linking European lead-country tranformation to U.S. transformation is crucial for achieving the dual goals of a stronger European defense *and* a stronger Atlantic Alliance.

The lead European countries already face requirements to perform stability operations, as emphasized in ESDP, as well as to make up deficits in their capabilities that have been identified by NATO, most recently through DCI. Meeting these short- and mid-term requirements will enable the core countries to contribute better to a range of noncombat and combat operations. However, as we have stressed, it will not suffice to achieve either transformation or effective cooperability. A demanding additional effort is needed.

We will look at what that additional effort might entail in the case of one crucial country: Germany. Having suggested in the previous chapter cooperable capabilities the United States might especially welcome from major allies, we now look at transformation and cooperability from a German vantage point, considering what Germany might want to do for its own reasons.

The State of Bundeswehr Reform

Germany has had to cope with a unique set of post–Cold War problems. It had little choice but to follow the general trend toward renationalization of force planning, owing to the declining effectivness of NATO's collective force planning in the absence of the Soviet threat. Unlike other European countries, however, Germany has been constrained by historical legacies and the need to consolidate its armed forces following unification. It had to overcome these constraints before the Bundeswehr could become a *mission-oriented* force, especially one oriented toward *international* missions.

Germany has been affected by the changing threat environment more than any other NATO ally. Throughout the Cold War, the Bundeswehr participated in NATO's defense of the Federal Republic; now, in the new era, Germany is seeking its proper role in multilateral operations to meet security responsibilities and threats outside the NATO Treaty area. The shift from territorial defense to an international-mission-oriented force, operating for extended periods at ever-greater distances, is a complex, often painful, process of learning and adjusting.

Its particular predicament notwithstanding, Germany has followed the United Kingdom, France, and other European allies in starting to reform its forces. The foundations were laid in 2000 with a set of decisions known as Bundeswehr Reform. Bundeswehr Reform is a step in the right direction: German forces are indeed being changed from a territorial defense force to a mission-oriented force. However, defining international missions is an especially sensitive political challenge for Germany. Because German politics have shied away from defining clear missions, especially those involving warfighting other than in self-defense, Bundeswehr planning is not yet based on an agreed-upon comprehensive strategic concept.

The Bundeswehr is, in principle, expected to prepare for missions across the full spectrum. However, the warfighting end of that spectrum is still undefined in national policy documents. As long as this is the case, Bundeswehr Reform will not generate the transformational capabilities needed for advanced expeditionary operations in coalition with U.S. and other lead-country forces.

Priority in Bundeswehr force planning has been given to "conflict prevention" and "crisis management," most likely in the Euro-Atlantic area. At the same time, Bundeswehr Reform does not rule out other missions, nor forces and equipment needed for possible use in other parts of the world. Thus, even the current reform accepts implicitly that the Bundeswehr may need to be equipped to participate as a coalition member in distant expeditionary combat. The events of 9/11 and their aftermath have brought such requirements to the surface of German public awareness, political debate, and military thinking.

Meanwhile, the Bundeswehr is reducing its size and base structure. Further streamlining to release resources for investment in transformation is both feasible and advisable given that a large portion of the force is not well suited for either international security missions or the new requirements of homeland defense. The Bundeswehr will have a *mission force* of 150,000 men. Thus, every second soldier will be in the mission force, compared to every sixth prior to Bundeswehr Reform.[24] It is further accepted already that the Bundeswehr must concentrate on *joint* capabilities and operations, as the United States and the United Kingdom are doing.

Increasingly, force planning for the Bundeswehr will now be *capability oriented*. It will seek joint solutions drawing upon six core capabilities: command and control, ISR, mobility, effective engagement, support and sustainability, and survivability. This approach is to be complemented by coordination and pooling of capabilities with Germany's European allies.

Bundeswehr Reform is sufficient to the extent it aims at capabilities for stability operations, which will remain an important German mission in any case. However, such capabilities fall well short of what is needed for cooperability with transformed U.S. forces in advanced expeditionary warfare. This does not mean that Bundeswehr Reform ought to be shelved. On the contrary, failure to implement it for any reason would undermine Germany's ability to perform even stability operations, as well as its credibility in NATO and the EU, and any hope that it can move beyond reform to transformation.

From Reform to Transformation

As we have argued, transformation is imperative if the Europeans are to increase their contribution to international peace, face up to rising threats worldwide, have strategic influence with the United States, and integrate with U.S. forces when U.S.-European interests and responsibilities dictate the use of deadly force. This applies to Germany no less than to the

---

[24]The issue of the total end-strength of the Bundeswehr is closely tied to the touchy issue of conscription, which implies large forces. Conscription is once again going to be the subject of a public debate, though without enough of a conceptual context as yet.

United Kingdom and France, notwithstanding their very different histories. It is therefore important to be thorough and clear about the limits of Bundeswehr Reform:

- The Bundeswehr is intended to have a continuum of capabilities for a wide spectrum of missions at its disposal. But it is already obvious, as foreshadowed by Operation Enduring Freedom, that the reform will not generate the capabilities needed for U.S.-led advanced expeditionary operations.
- The reform is focusing on current deficits identified by NATO and the EU, an approach that is more or less adequate for traditional operations. A more complex set of deficits must be identified relative to requirements for advanced expeditionary warfare. This, however, cannot be done based on actual operational experience, since the requirements must anticipate future threats and concepts of operation.
- The planned capabilities of the Bundeswehr are intended to cover short- and medium-term requirements. It is assumed that there will be several years available to prepare for threats that may emerge in the *long term*. However, this assumption of long warning time relates only to major invasion threats (where it may be valid in theory but is now irrelevant in reality). It is the wrong concept for the emerging threats for which Germany needs to be prepared—threats that require continuous transformation, not reconstitution.
- Indeed, threats resulting from the spread of WMD, as well as other asymmetric threats, may arise well before the "long term." The events on and following 9/11 assure there are greater challenges to come. This calls both for speeding up transformation and for making long-term planning an integral part of Bundeswehr planning.

- The philosophy of Bundeswehr Reform is to *evolve* German military capabilities—i.e., to replace existing platforms with more-modern ones of the same kind. However, some of the armament procurement projects favored today will require rethinking in light of transformation goals. More-radical changes from evolving Bundeswehr requirements will become imperative, as requirements already flowing from U.S. transformation suggest. Assuming Germany opts not to confine its forces to stability operations, it will have to learn—as the United States is having to learn—how to combine evolutionary modernization with leap-ahead needs.[25]

- Keeping a close watch on the U.S. transformation process will help to foster long-term planning for the Bundeswehr. However, mere observation and emulation will not suffice. The U.S. transformation process depends on wide-ranging concept development and experimentation. By connecting to the U.S. process, Bundeswehr planning can become more innovative and transformational, and German forces can become and remain cooperable with U.S. forces.

A German Approach to Tranformation

Germany needs a comprehensive approach to future development of the Bundeswehr that takes into account all three basic missions (see Chapter Three): stability operations, advanced expeditionary warfare, and homeland defense. This leads to two questions:

- Can the framework for transformation and cooperability laid out in Chapter Three serve as the basis for comprehensive German requirements?

---

[25]The tradeoff between evolutionary modernization procurement and leap-ahead investment is, of course, made less severe to the extent additional resources are made available for defense. As previously noted, the United States is able to do both because of its large and growing defense budget.

- Can the need to transform German forces for cooperability with U.S. forces in advanced expeditionary warfare flow naturally from Bundeswehr Reform?

Both questions can be answered in the affirmative. The Bundeswehr must continue to be able to conduct stability operations, including highly demanding ones, which will require continued modernization. At the same time, an additional effort must be made to plan and invest in transformed capabilities for advanced expeditionary operations. Planning such capabilities would in turn confront German planners with the need to achieve cooperability with U.S. forces, not only at the technical level, but also in doctrine, structures, preparations, and technological-industrial terms. Developing such transformed forces would enhance capabilities for stability operations while also strengthening the ability of German forces to cope with the fluid boundary between stability operations and combat.

Translating such a general approach into planned and ultimately actual capabilities will require a number of steps:

- A decision to make long-term planning an integral part of Bundeswehr Reform as a way of anticipating emerging threats and technological options.
- A detailed assessment of what German capabilities would complement U.S. forces in advanced warfighting (as illustrated in the previous chapter).
- An agreed-upon set of transformation criteria to guide German force planning.
- An initial evaluation of technologies that could provide these capabilities.
- Consultation with other core European force providers on a harmonized transformation effort.
- A broad understanding between the United States and Germany about linking Germany's transformation to the U.S. transformation process.

Germany should also perform an analysis of the military requirements associated with homeland defense, given that German participation in expeditionary operations could increase this requirement as well.

Preliminary Ideas on Transformed German Capabilities

Of the two options for European force transformation discussed earlier (see Chapter Four)—concentration on contributing throughout an operation (option 1) and concentration on areas of greatest impact (option 2)—the Bundeswehr should aim at providing the high-impact capabilities needed for option 2. This approach would contribute importantly both to coalition military effectiveness and to German influence on decisionmaking before, during, and after an operation. Such a German transformation strategy should be designed and pursued in coordination with the other leading European force providers, the goal being to create a sizable European contribution to U.S.-European expeditionary capabilities.

Certain candidate capabilities are obvious because they are already involved in current operations and have a demonstrated potential for improvement—e.g., SOF and chemical-biological-radiological-nuclear (CBRN) detection capabilities. Beyond these, the other U.S. preferences suggested for option 2 (again, see Chapter Four) are *all* worthy of serious German consideration. Some examples are worth elaborating.

German capabilities should focus especially on force enablers and force multipliers. In particular, ISR can provide force multiplication for the entire coalition—a single, mid-size airborne ISR platform might be worth a dozen fighters. It is unlikely that a U.S.-led coalition in expeditionary warfare could ever have *too much* ISR. ISR can also serve as a stimulant for transformation of other capabilities that can make use of improved situational awareness.

Once a preliminary German transformation plan has been developed, a systematic revision of existing modernization plans will be needed to identify capabilities that may lose their utility in the future or be replaceable by more-effective systems at lower cost and risk. For certain tasks, the potential of UAVs, compared to manned aircraft, is an important case in point.

There is, of course, a need to harmonize transformational investments as much as possible with those of the lead European allies and the United States. For example, sea-launched cruise missiles are increasingly effective as a tactical strike weapon. Because transformation requirements can be met nationally or within an allied framework, the German Navy might seek sea-launched cruise missile capabilities through a multinational program. Similarly, deployable missile defense will surely require a multinational approach. Finally, committing to a common C4ISTAR grid—essential for network-centric warfare—will not only lead to improved coalition capabilities but will also help tie together most aspects of transformation planning. This should be a high priority for Germany (and others).

In sum, German plans already in place to improve capabilities for stability operations form a good foundation. But they must be augmented by commitments to develop those capabilities Germany chooses to stress as it finds the role and specific tasks in coalition expeditionary warfare with which it is comfortable and for which it may even have a comparative advantage. With the U.S. transformation process as a beacon, the Bundeswehr should perform intensive concept development and experimentation (CDE) before making final investment decisions.

6 GETTING THE PROCESS RIGHT

A new, common U.S.-European military-mission framework, backed by political commitment and increased resources, would be an important accomplishment. However, it will not yield transformed and cooperable U.S. and European forces unless the implementation process is right. That process must tie together the force-planning processes of the United States and those of at the least the lead European force providers. We noted the inadequacies of the existing NATO and European processes earlier. Here we present them in more detail before prescribing an improved process.

Why Current Processes Are Inadequate

Force transformation challenges the status quo by calling for new, network-centric concepts, capabilities, and structures in order to preserve a capacity to project power despite the spread of anti-access threats. Cooperability demands that the United States and European allies sacrifice national freedom of action to build coalition capacity. These are strong strategic motivations, as they must be to impel tough decisions and determined implementation.

As already noted, previous initiatives and existing processes lack such strategic purposefulness. DCI was meant to implement NATO's "New Strategic Concept" (adopted at the 1999 Washington summit). But that concept was too vague to shape practical military planning, and in any case is inadequate for the post-9/11 world. It does not, for example, focus on expeditionary warfare against severe threats—including WMD, missiles, and terrorists—found mainly outside Europe. To the extent that there has been a strategic motivation within ESDP, it is to enable the Europeans to mount stability operations in or near Europe without U.S. involvement—i.e., to reduce European dependence on the United States. This motivation is fundamentally different from the goals of transformation and U.S.-European cooperability for expeditionary warfare against new, global threats.

Some European national planning has been more strategic: The British *Strategic Defence Review*, for example, called for military capabilities to enable the United Kingdom to serve as a "force for good in the world," implying full-spectrum operations alongside U.S. forces against all kinds of threats. But on the whole, the orientations of the leading European force providers have been ambiguous, especially toward expeditionary warfare far from Europe, and have had little relationship to each other, much less to the United States.

To some degree, this lack of strategic orientation is a consequence of the fact that European defense planning has been relatively shortsighted. U.S. transformation goals, as noted, stretch out 15 years and beyond. Yet even the United States has had difficulty reflecting these goals in short-to-mid-term modernization programs. Indeed, this critical link was largely missing in U.S. planning in the 1990s, which helps to explain why more progress was not made in transforming U.S. capabilities and why resources have continued to pour into capabilities that neither anticipate rising future threats nor exploit new technology. Increasingly, however, U.S. defense managers are setting milestones and benchmarks to link long- and short-term planning timeframes and thus to enable today's programs to be assessed in light of their long-term transformational value.

In contrast, neither DCI nor ECAP nor current European national force planning permits near-term choices to be viewed in light of their long-term utility, especially because strategic goals are so vague. A concentration on deficits in current capabilities will, at best, lead only to improvements for the short-to-mid term, ignoring both threats and technologies that can be anticipated.

Nor do existing processes connect top-down goals with bottom-up plans, which is crucial in transformation. DCI and ECAP reflect top-down decisions, which do not assure bottom-up progress among participating allies. In military transformation, as in endeavors to exploit information technology in other sectors, "micro" choices freely made by actors throughout an organization are what give life to a "macro" vision from the top. Not surprisingly, actual decisions taken in recent years by European defense managers have not been especially responsive to NATO or EU guidance, which helps to explain why the results have been so disappointing.

This problem is exacerbated by the fact that existing European force requirements tend not to flow from analysis of anticipated *operational* problems. Recent progress in U.S. transformation planning is largely the result of improved anticipation of operational challenges and solutions, as well as the related practice of "effects-based" planning. Such an operational focus is essential in creating the basis for common requirements that must underpin U.S.-European cooperability efforts.

Finally, multinational planning, whether in NATO or in the EU, typically suffers from ambiguity regarding how obligatory agreed-upon goals and measures are. Where sovereign nations are concerned, which of course remains the case in NATO and the EU, promises can be superceded by other national priorities. Awareness of this latitude can weaken the resolve of any one ally to implement tough decisions and can cause the entire collective "commitment" to unravel. (There are, however, specific cases in which real commitments have been made and kept, e.g., the successful

NATO AWACS program.) The lead European countries, being few in number, ought to be able to make broader commitments with confidence that they will be kept. Of the many reasons to focus on a relatively small set of agreed-upon priority measures, one is that compliance is more easily tracked. Moreover, tying together national force-planning processes will bring such commitments directly into national processes that allocate resources and set programmatic directions.

In sum, force-transformation planning must

- Be strategically purposeful
- Connect long-term needs to short-term programs
- Reflect both top-down and bottom-up ideas
- Be driven by operational challenges
- Be as obligatory as possible.

Although the U.S. transformation process is still young, it has these qualities. The goal is to impart them to European transformation as well, in ways that do not impair U.S. transformation and might actually improve it.

Concept Development and Experimentation: A Promising Avenue Toward Cooperability

To impart the needed qualities for allied force-transformation, and thus to achieve cooperability, the U.S.-European transformation process must tie *directly* into the planning, resource-allocation, and decisionmaking processes of each participant. Given the lead-country approach suggested above, this means that the transformation planning of the United Kingdom, France, and Germany must be tied directly into that of the United States. This could in turn set the stage for transformation planning for a larger group of NATO allies, as well as for the EU.

Given these requirements of effective implementation, we are especially enthused about the untapped potential of the existing CDE process. While CDE is inherently complex—for the United States by itself, let alone with European allies involved—increasing its role and effectiveness is a simple idea. The U.S. transformation process, as just noted, has the qualities needed for successful implementation. This is an especially good time to intensify U.S.-European CDE, because CDE efforts are already being intensified by the United States, reflecting the strong post-9/11 commitment to transform military concepts and capabilities. Indeed, failure to create a strong multilateral CDE at this stage will make it increasingly difficult for *any* U.S.-European transformation/cooperability effort to succeed.

Obstacles to this idea could arise on both sides of the Atlantic. In the United States, there could be a reluctance to burden further a process already complicated by the challenge of melding together the requirements and combat structures of the several armed services. U.S. planners are already wary of trying to achieve both U.S. jointness *and* U.S.-European cooperability concurrently. On the European side, there will be hesitation about being drawn into what appears to be an open-ended planning process without clearly stated targets, firm constraints, or regular political intervention. Europeans are more comfortable with disciplined, controllable planning, whereas the U.S. process tends to shift gears and directions easily based on internal logic rather than policy guidance. The very dynamism that is a virtue of U.S. transformation planning is going to be unsettling for the Europeans.

There could also be a concern among Europeans that being linked into U.S.-led CDE would compromise the goals of European independence in military requirements and capabilities. Undeniably, U.S.-European CDE would increase U.S.-allied military interdependence, which is, after all, the basic idea of cooperability. Presumably, European allies do not place their defense autonomy above the ability to conduct expeditionary warfare with the United States.

Notwithstanding these obstacles, multilateralizing CDE is a chance that must not be wasted. The United States may declare at Prague that it is determined to prepare with its allies for advanced coalition expeditionary warfare; but it is through CDE that this declaration can be put into practice and put to the test. The Europeans may proclaim at Prague that they are determined to transform their forces for such operations; but it is through CDE that such proclamations will become either reality or illusion. U.S. and European summiteers may agree that cooperability is imperative, and even identify high-priority capabilities; but cooperability will not happen unless the United States and Europe link their planning for advanced expeditionary warfare. CDE is the best way to do that.

CDE is a way of extending the U.S. transformation process, which is beginning to work, to the lead European allies, which need its impetus. It will bring into allied planning—national as well as collective—the qualities of strategic orientation, operational focus, short-to-long-term planning, and top-to-bottom synthesis.

At the same time, the challenges imposed by coalition operations will feed back through CDE into the U.S. force-planning process. This will complicate U.S. transformation planning, to be sure. However, to the extent that the United States is committed to a militarily effective Atlantic Alliance, it will face and overcome this additional challenge. Indeed, better to understand and fix the problems of coalition operations now than to wait until another crisis, only to discover then that the option has been foreclosed.

The United States might well discover that, beyond providing this strategic advantage, a linkage with allied transformation planning can actually stimulate and facilitate U.S. transformation planning. By focusing on selective critical tasks, allies often will find themselves at the leading edge of concept development, with the United States the beneficiary. Moreover, because their defense establishments are leaner to begin with, the lead European allies may find it easier and quicker than the United States to take certain transformation ideas from concept to capability. Involving lead allies can, in other words, make U.S. transformation more robust than it would be if it were purely a unilateral process.

In sum, CDE is a good way to hold both U.S. and European "feet to the fire." It presents the United States with the implications of a pledge to include allies in advanced expeditionary warfare, and it presents the allies with the implications of a pledge to build capabilities that merit their inclusion. It is also a good way to multilateralize creativity. Whereas the momentum of previous initiatives has tended to fade over time, CDE can help to ensure that the momentum of agreement at Prague will grow.

Implications for Institutions and Other Allies

The approach we offer in this report may leave the impression that it bypasses NATO, marginalizes allies other than the leading force providers, and disrupts ESDP. Undeniably, it could have such short-term effects. But it is the best way to achieve European transformation and U.S.-allied cooperability, which if not achieved will result in irreparable harm to NATO, ESDP, and all allies.

ESDP should have not one military purpose but two: stability operations *with or without* the United States, and advanced expeditionary operations *with* the United States anywhere U.S. and European common interests are threatened. The latter might be thought of as "ESDP II," though it cannot wait until the Europeans finish the business of assembling a force that can operate at the less-violent end of the spectrum without U.S. participation. The ultimate fulfillment of European global security aspirations must be to act as partner of the United States in the world, not to act independently of the United States in Europe.

Moreover, pursuit of transformation and cooperability would advance the goals of European cohesion and capabilities. As prescribed, this pursuit would demand that the lead European force providers harmonize their plans and forgo exclusive, or even competitive, bilateral arrangements to couple with U.S.-led force planning and operations. And it would give impetus to European investments to prepare for emerging threats and exploit emerging technologies. Simply put, if the forces of the lead European allies are made cooperable with those of the United States, they will surely be cooperable with each other.

What of NATO? Its force planning, decisionmaking, command structure, and operating doctrines have changed incrementally since the end of the Cold War, while changes in the global security environment have been sweeping. Adjustments in NATO's military plans are worked out through tedious diplomatic negotiations among professionals trained to avoid abrupt change. Consequently, the United States and the lead European allies do not presently rely on the NATO planning process to guide their force planning, and they cannot count on it to organize and guide their effort to create cooperable transformed forces.

NATO reform has been so slow in coming that it cannot be made a precondition of an urgent U.S.-European transformation/cooperability initiative, especially given the gathering speed of U.S. transformation. But NATO as an institution, as well as the majority of its members, will come along if the United States and the core European countries embark on the effort we have described. This effort should be neither exclusive nor automatically inclusive; it ought to be open to countries prepared to commit to and live by its results. However, the participation and leadership of the United States, Germany, France, and the United Kingdom are essential for setting the standard and prompting others to get on board.

Eventually, NATO can become the vital U.S.-European military alliance that sets relevant force goals, clarifies (rather than obfuscates) a common strategic outlook, adopts innovative military doctrines, organizes joint preparations, and actively maintains cooperability once it is attained. But that will be a NATO different from yesterday's, or today's.

7 CONCLUSIONS

This study suggests a number of prescriptions that can be adopted now:

- A new set of common strategic motivations for achieving cooperability between transformed U.S. and European forces.
- A common framework of military missions for identifying long-term requirements.
- A focus within that framework on advanced expeditionary warfare as the mission for which cooperability is most challenging and most vital, militarily and strategically.
- The several levels at which cooperability must be pursued.
- A European "lead-country" strategy as the starting point for transatlantic cooperability efforts.
- A practical mechanism—U.S.-allied CDE—that would link U.S. and European transformation planning and implementation.

This set of prescriptions provides an agenda for Prague. More specifically, the United States and the leading European force providers should commit to the following measures to achieve cooperability for advanced expeditionary warfare:

- Build core capabilities that are known, without further analysis, to constitute a minimum set of high-priority common requirements:
  - A common interoperable C4ISTAR grid
  - Major expansion of long-range airlift capacity

- Diverse tactical precision-strike platforms and weapons
- Ground forces that are rapidly deployable, theater mobile, and lighter but still lethal
- In-theater mobility for forces and logistics.
- On a national basis, have lead European allies concentrate on those capabilities beyond the core set that could contribute especially to the military effectiveness of coalition expeditionary warfare, even with some compromise of independence. We have illustrated such specialized tasks and capabilities. Ideally, the three largest European force providers—the United Kingdom, France, and Germany—would all soon have some notion of where they choose to concentrate, individually and together.
- Explore and implement common concepts of operation that stress rapid short-warning deployability, defeat of anti-access threats, integrated networked maneuver-and-strike operations, and creation of conditions for successful post-war stability operations.
- Work toward force structures, based on these concepts of operation, that make it possible for coalition forces to be tailored and integrated.
- Build programs for experimentation, simulation, training, and exercises that refine concepts of operation, capability requirements, and force structures, and, of course, prepare for integrated coalition operations.

Such steps would have purpose, focus, and depth, and would be feasible. They would make the most of what could be the final chance to create an effective U.S.-European military alliance for the new security era.

Assuming this chance is not lost, it should be understood that the effort has just begun. National force plans and investment programs will have to be reviewed and revised, informed by the multilateral CDE process. Resources will have to be reprogrammed and supplemented. Military education will have to be tuned to new concepts. The experience of actual operations will have to be absorbed. Analysis of new and anticipated threats will have to continue, and force plans will have to be adapted accordingly. Defense-industrial cooperation will have to be aligned with transformation and cooperability. Promising new technologies will have to be identified, developed, and shared.

In other words, the world will not stand still. 9/11 was a pivotal moment, but it does not freeze the future. Indeed, the United States and the European allies must be prepared for uncertainty, further change, and even new shocks. Many of the specific prescriptions offered here will surely require modification. What must not change is the conviction that the United States and the European allies must *prepare together* for whatever the future may hold.